Marking Out in Arabic

by Fethi Mansouri

TUTTLE Publishing

Tokyo | Rutland, Vermont | Singapore

Published by Tuttle Publishing, an imprint of Periplus Editions (HK) Ltd.

www.tuttlepublishing.com

ISBN 978-0-8048-3541-1

Distributed by:

North America, Latin America & Europe
Tuttle Publishing
364 Innovation Drive
North Clarendon, VT 05759-9436 USA
Tel: 1 (802) 773 8930
Fax: 1 (802) 773 6993
info@tuttlepublishing.com
www.tuttlepublishing.com

Japan
Tuttle Publishing
Yaekari Building, 3rd Floor
5-4-12 Osaki, Shinagawa-ku
Tokyo 141-0032
Tel: (81) 3 5437 0171
Fax: (81) 3 5437 0755
www.tuttle.co.jp

Asia Pacific
Berkeley Books Pte. Ltd.
61 Tai Seng Avenue #02-12
Singapore 534167
Tel: (65) 6280 1330
Fax: (65) 6280 6290
inquiries@periplus.com.sg
www.periplus.com

13 12 11 10
10 9 8 7 6 5

Printed in Singapore

Contents

Introduction

Making Out in Arabic is your passport to the living, breathing, colorful language spoken on the streets of the Arab world and the Middle East. It is the first book to give you access to the casual, unbuttoned Arabic that will allow you to express yourself in restaurants, cafes, and nightclubs, in crowded market places, and at train stations. Here you will find the warm-hearted language that you can use with friends, and also the rough-and-tumble language you can fall back on when you are ready for a fight.

Making Out in Arabic will be a useful companion throughout the Arab world – even when traveling in the furthest outbacks. So you want to meet people, make friends, eat out, go dancing, or just take part in friendly chitchat? A quick glance at *Making Out in Arabic* and you'll have the language at your fingertips.

PRONUNCIATION

Consonants

The imitated pronunciation should be read as if it were English. The emphatic consonants *d* and *t*, *s* and *z* represent more a question of volume than a separate sound.

th is pronounced like **th** in **th**ree;
dh is pronounced like **th** in **th**ere.
kh is pronounced like **ch** in Scottish lo**ch**;
gh is the voiced equivalent.

A few sounds do not exist in English, such as the uvular stop (q), which is pronounced like a "k" in the back of one's throat; a glottal stop ('), an abrupt, momentary cutting off of air followed by an explosive release and the pharyngeal fricatives both voiced (') and voiceless (h). A voiced pharyngeal fricative is produced by forcing air through a narrow channel in the back of the throat with vibrations at one's vocal chords while a voiceless one is produced in the same manner without vibrations at the vocal chords. To check if a sound is voiced, place your fingers on your throat and feel the vibrations.

Vowels

There are three basic short vowels in Arabic and three long ones. These are:

a as in c**a**t
aa as in f**a**r
i as in p**i**n
ii as in cl**ea**n
u as in p**u**t
uu as in n**oo**n

Stress

Arabic words do not have a stress accent in the way that English ones do. However, individual consonants can exhibit stress by means of doubling. For example, in the word ***kassara*** "to break," the double s indicates consonantal stress as in the English name "Cassandra."

PRONOUNS

The following are the main Arabic personal pronouns:

I	***anaa***
You (singular, masculine)	***anta***
You (singuar, feminine)	***anti***
He	***huwa***
She	***hiya***
We	***nah̲nu***
You (plural, masculine)	***antum***
You (plural, feminine)	***antunna***
They	***hum***

QUESTIONS

The easiest way of asking a question in Arabic is to use a question word at the beginning of the phrase or sentence, e.g.:

What's this?	***maa*** ***haadha?***
Which man?	***ayyu*** ***rajul?***
Which lady?	***ayyatu*** ***imra'a?***
Who are you?	***man*** ***anta?***
Why did the girl leave?	***limaadhaa*** ***kharajat al-bintu?***
When did the plane land?	***mataa*** ***habatat at-taa'ira?***
Where did he buy a shirt?	***ayna*** ***ishtaraa qamiis?***

An affirmative sentence (statement) may be turned into an interrogative one (question) by means of the word ***hal***, e.g.:

The boy ate	***akala al-waladu***
Did the boy eat?	***hal*** ***akala al-waladu?***

NEGATION

Negation is expressed differently for nominal as opposed to verbal sentences.

When negating nominal and adjectival phrases, ***laysa*** or one of its variants is inserted after the noun or pronoun to which it refers, e.g:

I am not angry ***lastu*** ***ghaadiban*** (literally "not I angry")

Laysa combines with the personal pronouns as follows:

I	***lastu***
You (singular, masculine)	***lasta***
You (singuar, feminine)	***lasti***
He	***laysa***
She	***laysat***
We	***lasnaa***
You (plural, masculine)	***lastum***

You (plural, feminine)	***lastunna***
They	***laysuu***

In addition, there are four verbal negation words used according to the tense of the verb, e.g.:

laa	present	***laa ashrab***	I'm not drinking
lan	future	***lan ashrab***	I won't drink
lam	past	***lam ashrab***	I didn't drink
maa	past/continuing	***maa sharibtu***	I haven't drunk

What's Up? 1

Hello. — marhaban
مرحبا

How are you? — kayfa l-haal?
كيف الحال؟

I'm fine. — bikhayr
بخير

OK, I guess. — al-umuur 'aadiyya
الأمور عادية
Not very common in Arabic.

So-so. — laa ba'sa
لا بأس

Things are busy. — anaa mashghuul jiddan
أنا مشغول جدا

Things are hard. — al-awdaa' sa'ba
الأوضاع صعبة

Literally, this means the situation (conditions) is not as good as it should be.

How have you been? — kayfa anta?
كيف أنت؟

I've been fine, thank you. — anaa bikhayr, shukran
أنا بخير، شكرا

What's new? — hal min jadiid?
هل من جديد؟

What have you been doing? — maadha kunta taf'al?
ماذا كنت تفعل؟

Nothing much. — laysa kathiiran
ليس كثيرا

Nothing special.
لا شيء يذكر
laa shay' yudhkar

I haven't seen you around for a while.
لم أرك في المنطقة منذ فترة
lam arak fi l-mintaqa mundhu fitra

Yes, it's been a long time.
نعم، لقد مضى وقت طويل
na'am, laqad mada waqtun tawiil

Have you been around?
هل كنت في المنطقة؟
Hal kunta fi l-mintaqa?

What are you doing here?
ماذا تفعل هنا؟
maadha taf'al hunaa

How's Peter / Mary doing?
كيف حال بيتر/ماري؟
kayfa haal Peter / Mary?

He's / she's fine.
إنه/إنها بخير
innahu / innaha bikhayr

Anything new with Peter/ Mary?
هل من جديد مع بيتر/ماري؟
hal min jadiid ma'a Peter / Mary?

What's wrong?
ماذا حدث؟
maadha hadath?

What's on your mind?
ماذا يدور بفكرك؟
maadha yaduur bifikrik?

Nothing.
لا شيء
laa shay'

I was just thinking.
كنت أفكر
kuntu ufakkir

I was just daydreaming.
لقد سرحت بالتفكير
laqad sarihtu bit-tafkiir

It's none of your business.
هذا الأمر لا يهمك
haadha al-amr laa yahummuk

Mind your own business. ihtamm bimaa huwa min sha'nik
اهتم بما هو من شأنك

Leave me alone. utruknii liwahdii
اتركني لوحدي

Go away. idhhab min hunaa
إذهب من هنا

Fuck off. hill 'annii
حل عني

This is a colloquial expression which means "get out of my sight". The actual expression "fuck off" is not used in Standard Arabic.

Really? haqqan?
حقا ؟

Is that so? ahaakadhaa?
أهكذا ؟

Are you sure? hal anta muta'akkid?
هل أنت متأكد ؟

Oh, yeah? aah, na'am?
أه، نعم؟

You're lying. anta takdhib
أنت تكذب

This expression is very impolite in Arabic and should be avoided as much as possible. You can suggest to your interlocutor instead that their information might be incorrect using the expression "ma'luumatik khaatia".

Don't lie. laa takdhib
لا تكذب

Stop lying. tawaqqaf 'an il-kadhib
توقف عن الكذب

How come? wa kayfa dhaalik?
وكيف ذلك؟

What do you mean? maadha taqsid?
مذا تقصد؟

Is something wrong? maa l-mushkila?
ما المشكلة؟

What's the difference? maa l-farq?
ما الفرق؟

What? maadha?
ماذا؟

Huh? haa?
ها؟

Are you serious? hal anta jiddii?
هل أنت جدي؟

You don't mean it! anta laa taqsid haadha!
أنت لا تقصد هذا!

That's impossible! haadha mustahiil!
هذا مستحيل!

That's too good to be true. laa yumkin an yakuun haadha sahiihan
لا يمكن أن يكون هذا صحيحا

I don't believe it. laa usaddiq haadha
لا أصدق هذا

You're joking.
أنت تمزح
anta tamzah

Are you making fun of me?
هل تسخر مني؟
hal taskhar minnii?

Stop joking!
توقف عن المزاح!
tawaqqaf 'an il-muzaah!

I'm not joking.
لست أمزح
lastu amzah

It's true.
هذا صحيح
haadha sahiih

You're crazy.
أنت مجنون
anta majnuun

That's right.
هذا صحيح
haadha sahiih

Absolutely.
بالتأكيد
bit-ta'kiid

Definitely.
قطعا
qat'an

Of course. tab'an
طبعا

You'd better believe it. 'alayka an tusaddiq
عليك أن تصدق

No way. laa yumkin
لا يمكن
The expression "mustahiil" meaning "impossible" can also be used in this context.

I guess so. azunnu dhaalik
أظن ذلك

I hope so. aamulu dhaalik
آمل ذلك

I hope not. aamulu an laa yakuuna kadhaalik
آمل أن لا يكون كذلك

It might be true. mumkin an yakuun haqiiqa
ممكن أن يكون حقيقة

I doubt it. ashukku fii dhaalik
أشك في ذلك

I don't think so. laa azunnu dhaalik
لا أظن ذلك

I'm not sure. lastu muta'akkidan
لست متأكدا

There's no way of knowing. laysa hunaaka tariiqa lilma'rifa
ليس هناك طريقة للمعرفة

I can't say for sure. laa astatii' an ua'kkid
لا أستطيع أن أوكد

I wonder... atasaa'alu...
أتساءل...
The literal meaning of "I wonder" in Arabic is "ata'ajjabu" which indicates astonishment rather the English sense of "wondering" about something.

Forget it. insaa
إنسى

I've had enough.
تحملت كفاية
tahammaltu kifaaya

Damn.
اللعنة
al-la'na

Bullshit.
هذا هراء
haadha huraa'

You can't do that.
لا تستطيع أن تفعل ذلك
laa tastatii' an taf'al dhaalika

I don't care.
لا يهمني
laa yahummuniil

It's got nothing to do with me.
لا علاقة لي بذلك
laa 'alaaqata lii bidhaalik

It means nothing to me.
لا يعني شيئا بالنسبة لي
laa ya'nii shay-an bin-nisbati lii

I'm not interested.
لا يهمني
laa yahummunii

Sure, if you like.
بالتأكيد، إذا رغبت
bit-ta'kiid, idhaa raghibt

Whatever you want.
كما تريد
kamaa turiid

Anything's fine with me.
أنا لا أكترث لذلك
anaa laa aktarith lidhaalik

I think so too.
أظن ذلك أيضا
azunnu dhaalika aydan

So am I. / Me too.
وكذلك أنا/أنا أيضا
wa kadhaalika anaa / anaa aydan

I see what you mean.
أنا أرى ما تقصده
anaa ara maa taqsiduhu

All right, I understand.
حسنا، أنا أفهم
hasanan, anaa afham

All right, no problem.
حسنا ، لا يوجد أي إشكال
hasanan, laa yuujad ayy ishkaal

That was good.
كان ذلك جيدا
kaana dhaalika jayyidan

Great!
عظيم
'aziim

I like it!
هذا يعجبني
haadha yu'jibunii!

I did it!
لقد فعلتها
laqad fa'altuhaa

No problem.
ما من مشكلة
maa min mushkila

It was no problem.
لم يكن صعبا
lam yakun sa'ban

But...
ولكن...
wa laakin...

It's risky.
هذا أمر خطير
haadha amrun khatiir

The word "risky" translates to "dangerous" in Arabic which is not used unless the situation is indeed "dangerous". A suitable alternative is the word "muhim" meaning literally "important" but one that coveys the English meaning of "serious" adequately.

Cheer up. إبتهج	ibtahij
Calm down. إهدأ	ihda'
Never mind. ليس مهما	laysa muhimman
It doesn't matter. لا يهم	laa yahumm

Basic Phrases 2

Yes. na'am
نعم

No. laa
لا

OK. tayyib
طيب

This word can be used interchangeably with the word "hasanan", meaning "well".

What? maadha?
ماذا ؟

Who? man?
من ؟

Whose? liman?
لمن ؟

Where? ayna?
أين ؟

When? mataa?
متى ؟

Why? limaadha?
لماذا ؟

Why not? limaa laa?
لم لا ؟

Because... li'anna...
لأن...

How? kayfa?
كيف ؟

This. — haadha
هذا

That. — dhaaka
ذاك

Here. — hunaa
هنا

There. — hunaaka
هناك

Maybe. — mumkin
ممكن

Maybe not. — rubbamaa laa
ربما لا

I. — anaa
أنا

You. — anta
أنت

He / she. — huwa / hiya
هو/هي

We. — nahnu
نحن

You (plural). — antum
أنتم

They. — humm
هم

Don't. — laa taf'al
لا تفعل

Please. — min fadlik
من فضلك

The expression "law samaht" meaning "if you permit" can be used interchangeably here.

Thank you. — shukran
شكرا

Can I have that?
ممكن آخذ ذلك؟
mumkin aakhudh dhaalika?

How much is this?
بكم هذا؟
bikamm haadha?

That's so cheap.
هذا رخيص
haadha rakhiis

That's not cheap.
هذا ليس رخيصا
haadha laysa rakhiisan

That's too expensive.
هذا غال جدا
haadha ghaalin jiddan

I'm not buying that.
لن أشتري ذلك
lan ashtariya dhaalika

Make it cheaper and I'll buy it.
إذا ترخص الثمن فسأشترية
idhaa turakhkhis ath-thaman fa-sa-ashtariih

Bargaining is normal in most Arabic countries especially in old markets (souks) and medinas.

Got a Minute? 3

One moment, please. lahza min fadlik
لحظة من فضلك

When? mataa?
متى؟

Till when? ila ghaayat?
إلى غاية...؟

About when? mataa taqriiban?
متى تقريبا؟

The Arabic question word "mataa" can also be used in this context.

What time? fii ayy waqt?
في أي وقت؟

Is that too early? hal haadhaa baakirun jiddan?
هل هذا باكر جدا؟

Is that too late? hal haadha muta'akhirun jiddan?
هل هذا متأخر جدا؟

What time is it convenient for you?
ما هو الوقت المناسب لك؟
maa huwa al-waqt al-munaasib laka?

What day is it convenient for you?
أي يوم مناسب لك؟
ay yawm munaasib laka?

How about tomorrow?
ما رأيك في الغد؟
maa ra'yuk fi l-ghad?

How about the day after tomorrow?
ما رأيك في بعد الغد؟
maa ra'yuka fii ba'd al-ghad?

Today.
اليوم
al-yawm

Yesterday.
البارحة
al-baariha

In many Arabic countries "amsi" will be used.

The day before yesterday
أول أمس
awwal ams

How about the 18th?
ما رأيك في الثامن عشر؟
maa ra'yuk fii ath-thaamin 'ashar?

The first / second / third / fourth / fifth...
ألأول/الثاني/الثالث/الرابع/الخامس
al-awwal / ath-thaanii / ath-thaalith / ar-raabi' / al-khaamis

The sixth / seventh / eighth / ninth / tenth...
السادس/السابع/الثامن/التاسع/العاشر
as-saadis / as-saabi' / ath-thaamin / at-taasi' / al-'aashir

The eleventh / twelfth / thirteenth / fourteenth / fifteenth...
الحادي عشر/الثاني عشر/الثالث عشر/الرابع عشر/الخامس عشر
al-haadii 'ashar / ath-thaanii 'ashar / ath-thaalith 'ashar / ar-raabi' 'ashar / al-khaamis 'ashar

The sixteenth / seventeenth / eighteenth / nineteenth / twentieth...

السادس عشر/السابع عشر/الثامن عشر/التاسع عشر/العشرون

as-saadis 'ashar / as-saabi' 'ashar / ath-thaamin 'ashar / at-taasi' 'ashar / al-'ishruun

The twenty-first / twenty-second / twenty-third / twenty-fourth / twenty-fifth...

الحادي والعشرون/الثاني والعشرون/الثالث والعشرون/الرابع والعشرون/الخامس والعشرون

al-haadi wal 'ishruun / ath-thaani wal 'ishruun / ath-thaalith wal 'ishruun / ar-raabi' wal 'ishruun / al-khaamis wal 'ishruun

The twenty-sixth / twenty-seventh / twenty-eighth / twenty-ninth...

السادس والعشرون/السابع والعشرون/الثامن والعشرون/التاسع والعشرون

as-saadis wal 'ishruun / as-saabi' wal 'ishruun / ath-thaamin wal 'ishruun / at-taasi' wal 'ishruun

The thirtieth / thirty-first...

الثلاثون/الواحد والثلاثون

ath-thalaathuun / al-waahid wath-thalaathuun

...of January / February / March / April / May / June / July.

من كانون الثاني/شباط/آذار/نيسان/أيار/حزيران/تموز

min kaanuun ath-thaanii / shubaat / aadhaar / naysaan / ayyar / huzayraan / tammuuz

In many parts of the Arab world, different names for the calendar months are in use. For example, in North Africa the French names of months are Arabised.

...of August / September / October / November / December.

من آب/أيلول/تشرين الأول/تشرين الثاني/كانون الأول

min aab / ayluul / tishriin al-awwal / tishriin ath-thaanii / kaanuun al-awwal

Could it be sooner?
ممكن أن نقدم موعده؟
mumkin an nuqaddim maw'idah?

I'd rather make it later.
أفضل تأخيره
ufaddil ta'khiirah

One / two / three / four / five / six o'clock.
الساعة الواحدة/الثانية/الثالثة/الرابعة/الخامسة/السادسة
as-saa'a al-waahida / ath-thaaniya / ath-thaalitha / ar-raabi'a / al-khaamisa / as-saadisa

Half past seven / eight / nine / ten / eleven.
السابعة والنصف/الثامنة/التاسعة/العاشرة/الحادية عشرة
as-saabi'a wan-nisf / ath-thaamina / at-taasi'a / al-'aashira / al-haadiyata 'ashara

In the morning.
في الصباح
fi s-sabaah

In the afternoon.
بعد الظهر
ba'da z-zuhr

In the evening.
في المساء
fi l-masaa'

Midday.
منتصف النهار
muntasaf an-nahaar

Midnight.
منتصف الليل
muntasaf al-layl

Then when can you make it?
إذا متى تستطيع أن تقوم بة؟
idhaa mataa tastatii' an taquum bihi?

What time can I come over?
متى أستطيع أن أتي إليك؟
mataa astatii' an aati ilayka?

What time do we leave?
متى سنغادر؟
mataa sa-nughaadir?

What time do we arrive?
متى سنصل؟
mataa sanasil?

What time will you be back?
في أي وقت تعود ؟
fii ay waqt ta'uud?

Are you ready?
هل أنت مستعد ؟
hal anta musta'idd?

When will you do it?
متى ستقوم به؟
mataa sataquumu bihi?

When will it be finished?
متى سينتهي؟
mataa sa-yantahii?

How long will it take?
كم من الوقت يحتاج؟
kam mina al-waqt yahtaaj?

It'll be done soon.
سأنتهي قريبا
sa-antahii qariiban

Not now.
ليس الآن
laysa al'aan

Maybe later.
ممكن فيما بعد
mumkin fiimaa ba'd

Not yet.
ليس بعد
laysa ba'd

Last time.
آخر مرة
aakhir marra

Previously.
سابقا
saabiqan

Next time.
المرة القادمة
al-marra al-qaadima

I don't know when.
لا أعرف متى
laa a'rif mataa

I don't know yet.
لا أعلم بعد
laa a'lam ba'd

I'm not sure.
لست متأكدا
lastu muta'akkidan

Sometime. ahyaanaan
أحيانا

Someday. yawman maa
يوما ما

Always. daa'iman
دائما

Every day. kulla yawm
كل يوم

Never again! lan yu'aad!
لن يعاد

Anytime is fine. mumkin fii ayy waqt
ممكن في أي وقت

You decide when. anta tuqarrir mataa
أنت تقرر متى

Whenever you like. mataa yahlu lak
متى يحلو لك

That day is fine. dhaalika al-yawm munaasib
ذلك اليوم مناسب

OK, let's meet then. tayyib, fa-lnaltaqii idhan
طيب، فلنلتقي إذا

That's a bad day for me. haadhaa yawm sayyi' lii (laa yunaasibnii)
هذا يوم سيئ لي (لا يناسبني)

Arab people don't always state such "negative" opinions directly.

Let's begin. hayyaa nabda'
هيا نبدأ

Let's continue. hayya nutaabi'
هيا نتابع

Let's start again. hayya nabda' marra ukhra
هيا نبدأ مرة أخرى

Let's do it later. fa-lnaqum bihi laahiqan
فلنقم به لاحقا

It'll only take a minute.
سيأخذ لحظة فقط
saya'khudh lahza faqat

Hurry up!
أسرع
asri'!

Do it later.
قم به لاحقا
qum bihi laahiqan

I'll do it quickly.
سأقوم به بسرعة
sa-aquum bihi bi-sur'a

I'll finish soon.
سأنتهي حالا
sa-antahii haalan

I've finished.
انتهيت
intahaytu

Have you finished?
هل انتهيت؟
hal intahayta?

Hey There! 4

Listen! isma’

إسمع!

An interrogative version of the verb in this situation will also be appropriate as in: “hal tasma’ shayan?”

Can you hear something? hal tasma’ shay-an?

هل تسمع شيئا ؟

What’s that noise? maa haadhihi ad-dajja?

ما هذه الضجة؟

Listen to what I’m saying. isghi limaa aquuluh

إصغ لما أقوله

Don’t listen to him. laa tastami’ ilayh

لا تستمع إليه

Don’t ask me that. laa tas'alnii

لا تسألني

Can you hear me? hal tasma’nii?

هل تسمعني؟

Did you hear me? hal sami’tanii?

هل سمعتني؟

I couldn't hear.
لم أسمع
lam asma'

I don't want to hear about that.
لا أريد أن أسمع عن ذلك
laa uriid an asma' 'an dhaalik

Say something.
قل شيئا
qul shay-an

Don't say such things.
لا تقل شيئا كذلك
laa taqul shay-an kadhaalik

What are you talking about?
عما تتكلم؟
'ammaa tatakallam?

You shouldn't say things like that.
يجب ألا تقول مثل تلك الأشياء
yajib allaa taquul mithil tilka al-ashyaa'

I didn't say anything.
لم أقل شيئا
lam aqul shay-an

Let's talk in Arabic.
هيا نتكلم بالعربية
hayyaa natakallam bil-'arabiyya

Can you speak Arabic?
أتستطيع أن تتحدث بالعربية؟
atastatii' an tatahadath bil-'arabiyya?

Arab people always find it strange that foreigners are able to speak Arabic (even someone with a very basic competence level).

Let's carry on talking.
لنستمر في الحديث
li-nastamirr fil-hadiith

Let's talk about it later.
فلنتكلم عن ذلك لاحقا
fa-li-natakallam 'an dhaalika laahiqan

Tell me later.
أخبرني لاحقا
akhbirnii laahiqan

I don't feel like talking.
لا أرغب في الكلام
laa arghab fil-kalaam

I don't want to talk to you.
لا أريد أن أتكلم معك
laa uriid an atakallam ma'aka

Don't ask me that.
لا تسألني
laa tas'alnii

I don't want to talk about it.
لا أريد أن أتحدث عن ذلك
laa uriid an atahaddath 'an dhaalik

Don't make excuses.
لا تختلق أعذار
laa takhtaliq a'dhaaran

That's not a good excuse.
هذا ليس عذرا مقبولا
haadha laysa 'udhran maqbuulan

Stop complaining.
توقف عن التشكي
tawaqqaf 'an il-tashakki

Complaining about little things is common in Arabic culture, in particular among women.

Do you know what you're saying?
هل تدرك ما تقول؟
hal tudrik maa taquul?

Don't talk so loudly.
لا تتكلم بصوت مرتفع
laa tatakallam bisawt murtafi'

Speak up. irfa' sawtak
إرفع صوتك

Speak more slowly. tahaddath bihuduu'
تحدث بهدوء

Say it again. a'id maa qult
أعد ما قلت

Do you understand? atafham?
أتفهم؟

I understand. anaa afham
أنا أفهم

I don't understand. lam afham
لم أفهم

Can you understand me? atastatii' an tafhamnii?
أتستطيع أن تفهمني؟

I couldn't understand. lam astati' an afham
لم أستطع أن افهم

What did you say? maadha qult?
ماذا قلت؟

Did you say that? hal qulta dhaalik?
هل قلت ذلك؟

I didn't say that. lam aqul dhaalik
لم أقل ذلك

I didn't say anything. lam aqul shay-an
لم أقل شيئا

I didn't tell anyone. lam ukhbir ahadan
لم أخبر أحدا

I won't tell anyone. lan ukhbira ahadan
لن أخبر أحدا

Look At That! 5

Look! unzur!
أنظر

Look at this. unzur ila haadha
أنظر إلى هذا

Look at that. unzur ila dhaalika
أنظر إلى ذلك

Take a look. ilqi nazra
إلق نظرة

Normally such utterances would be followed by the adverb "bi-sur'a" meaning quickly.

Don't look! laa tanzur!
لا تنظر

Don't look at this / that. laa tanzur ila haadha / dhaalika
لا تنظر إلى هذا/ذلك

Can you see it? hal taraah?
هل تراه؟

Did you see it?
هل رأيته؟
hal ra'aytah?

I can see it clearly.
إني أرى ذلك بوضوح
innii araa dhaalika bi-wuduuh

I saw it.
رأيته
ra'aytuhu

I didn't see it.
لم أره
lam arah

I don't want to see it.
لا أريد أن أراه
laa uriid an araah

Have you seen Jeff?
هل رأيت جيف؟
hal ra'ayta Jeff?

I want to see you soon.
أريد أن أراك قريبا
uriidu an araaka qariiban

The term "qariiban" means literally "near" but as in this context it can also indicate temporal proximity.

I've been wanting to see you.
لقد اردت رؤيتك منذ وقت طويل
laqd ardtu ru'yataka mundhu waqtin tawiilin

I saw Paul the other day.
رأيت بول قبل بضعة أيام
ra'aytu buul qabla bid'at ayyaam

I'm going to see Kim next week.
سوف أرى كيم في الأسبوع القادم
sawfa araa Kim fil-'usbuu' al-qaadim

So we meet again!
إذا نلتقي مرة أخرى
idhan naltaqii marra ukhraa!

I'll show you.
سوف أريك
sawfa uriik

I won't show you.
لن أريك
lan uriika

Coming and Going 6

Come here! ta’aala hunaa
تعال هنا

Such commands should always be preceded by polite expressions such as “min fadlik” meaning “please”.

Come over to my place. ta’aala ila baytii
تعال إلى بيتي

I’ll come over soon. sa-azuuruk qariiban
سأزورك قريبا

Come later. zurnii laahiqan
زرني لاحقا

Can you come? atastatii’ an ta'tii?
أتستطيع أن تأتي؟

Come along with us. ta’aala ma’anaa
تعال معنا

She’s coming here. innaha aatiya ila huna
إنها آتية إلى هنا

I’m coming, wait a second. ana aatin, intazir lahza
أنا أت، إنتظر لحظة

I’ll go soon. sa-adhhabu haalan
سأذهب حالا

I can go. astatii’ an adhhab
أستطيع أن أذهب

I think I can go. a’taqid annahu bi-imkaanii an adhhaba
أعتقد أنه بإمكاني أن أذهب

I can’t go. laa astatii’ an adhhaba
لا أستطيع أن أذهب

I want to go.
أريد أن أذهب
uriid an adhhab

I want to go to Baghdad.
أريد أن أذهب إلى بغداد
uriid an adhhaba ila baghdaad

I really want to go.
في الواقع أريد أن أذهب
fil-waaqi' uriid an adhhaba

I don't want to go.
لا أريد أن أذهب
laa uriid an adhhaba

I really don't want to go.
في الواقع لا أريد أن أذهب
fil-waaqi' laa uriid an adhhaba

You're going, aren't you?
أنت ذاهب أليس كذلك؟
anta dhaahib alaysa kadhaalika?

You went, didn't you?
ذهبت أليس كذلك؟
dhahabta alaysa kadhaalika?

I'm going.
أنا ذاهب
anaa dhaahib

I'm not going.
لست ذاهبا
lastu dhaahiban

I went.
ذهبت
dhahabtu

I didn't go.
لم أذهب
lam adhhab

Don't go!
لاتذهب
laa tadhhab

Don't go yet.
لا تذهب بعد
laa tadhhab ba'd

I have to go.
يجب أن أذهب
yajib an adhhab

I must go now.
يجب أن أذهب الآن
yajib an adhhab al-aan

May I go?
هل أستطيع أن أذهب؟
hal astatii' an adhhab?

Shall we go?
هل نذهب؟
hal nadhhab?

Let's go.
هيا بنا
hayyaa binaa

Let's leave here.
لنترك هنا
li-natruk hunaa

I'm leaving soon.
أنا مغادر قريبا
anaa mughaadirun qariiban

She has left here.
لقد غادرت هذا المكان
laqad ghaadarat haadha l-makaan

Stay here.
إبق هنا
ibqa hunaa

Where are you going?
إلى أين ذاهب؟
ila ayna dhaahib?

Please go first.
أرجوك أذهب أنت أولا
arjuuk idhhab anta awwalan

Thanks for letting me go first.
شكرا على سماحك لي بالذهاب أولا
shukran 'ala samaahika lii bi-dhahaab awwalan

Go slowly.
تمهل
tamahhal

Eat, Drink, Be Merry! 7

I'm hungry.
أنا جائع
anaa jaa'i'

Food and eating are major social events in the Arab world. Even a quick lunch can be a social event shared among friends and family members.

I'm starving.
أنا جوعان
anaa jaw'aan

I'd like to eat something.
أريد أن أكل شيئا ؟
uriidu an aakula shay-an

Have you eaten?
هل أكلت؟
hal akalta?

Joining others and sharing food with them is a sign of welcome and friendship.

I haven't eaten yet.
لم آكل بعد
lam aakul ba'd

Do you want to eat something?
أتريد أن تأكل شيئا ؟
aturiid an ta'kula shay-an?

I don't want to eat.
لا أريد أن آكل
laa uriid an aakul

I won't eat.
لن آكل
lan aakula

It is important to indicate the reason for not wanting to eat, otherwise a negative conclusion can be drawn.

Do you want to eat some more?
هل تريد المزيد من الطعام؟
hal turiid al-maziid min at-ta'am?

It is customary to show that you really enjoyed the food by accepting an extra serving.

What would you like?
ماذا تحب؟
maadha tuhibb?

I'm thirsty.
أنا عطشان
anaa 'atshaan

Do you want to drink something?
هل تريد أن تشرب شيئا؟
hal turiidu an tashraba shay-an?

I'd like to drink beer.
أحب أن أشرب بيرة
uhibbu an ashraba biira

Beer is not consumed publicly in many Arab countries because of the strict Islamic rules. But many young people do often drink beer in hotels and western-style cafes (bars).

I want some liquor.
أريد بعض الشراب
uriidu ba'd ash-sharaab

I don't want to drink.
لا أريد أن أشرب
laa uriidu an ashraba

I won't drink.
لن أشرب
lan ashraba

I haven't drunk yet.
لم أشرب بعد
lam ashrab ba'd

This tastes too weird.
طعمه غريب جدا
ta'muhu ghariib jiddan

I think this has gone bad.
أظن أنه تالف
azunnu annahu taalif

I think this stuff's stale.
أظن أن هذا الأكل قديم
azunnu anna haadhaa al-akil qadiim

Wow, this tastes good!
هذا طعمه جيد
haadhaa, ta'mahu jayyid!

Do you want to drink some more?
أتريد المزيد من الشراب؟
aturiid al-maziid mina ash-sharaab?

Thank you, but I still have some.
شكرا ، ولكن ما زال لدي بعض الشراب
shukran, wa laakin maa zaala laday ba'du ush-sharaab

Come on, drink a little bit more.
هيا ، أشرب المزيد
hayya, ishrab il-maziid

It's on me.
على حسابي
'ala hisaabii

Unlike in Western societies, Arabs do not like to divide the bill. So one individual (usually the host) will always pay the full bill.

How about some dinner?
ما رأيك في تناول العشاء معا؟
maa ra'yuka fii tanaawul al-'ashaa' ma'an?

Have you ordered?
هل طلبت؟
hal talabt?

Is the meal ready?
هل الوجبة جاهزة (حاضرة)؟
hal al-wajba jaahiza (haadira)?

It's ready.
إنها جاهزة
innaha jaahiza

Will you try this food?
ممكن أن تتذوق هذا الطعام؟
mumkin an tatadhawwaq haadha at-ta'aam?

That looks delicious.
يبدو لذيذا
yabduu ladhiidhan

It smells good.
رائحته جيدة
raai'hatuhu jayyida

This is a feast.
هذه وليمة
haadhihi waliima

Yum!
لذيذ
ladhiidh!

Do you want more food?
اتريد المزيد من الطعام؟
aturiid al-maziid mina at-ta'aam?

I'd like more food.
أحب المزيد من الطعام
uhib al-maziid mina at-ta'aam

Give me some more.
أعطني المزيد من الطعام
a'tinii al-maziid mina at-ta'aam

Give me a little more.
أعطني أقل من هذا
a'tinii aqal min haadha

Enough?
أيكفي؟
ayakfii?

Enough.
يكفي
yakfii

Not enough.
لا يكفي
laa yakfii

What's this?
ما هذا؟
maa haadhaa?

Taste it.
تذوقه
tadhawwaqhu

I can't eat that.
لا أستطيع أن آكل هذا
laa astatii' an aakula haadhaa

What's it called?
ماذا يسمى؟
maadhaa yusammaa?

Is it spicy?
هل هو مبهر؟
hal huwa mubahharr?

Yuck!
إخ (مقرف)
ikh (muqrif)!

It's not good.
ليس جيدا
laysa jayyidan

It doesn't taste good.
طعمه ليس جيدا
ta'muhu laysa jayyidan

It's awful.
إنه فظيع
innahu fazii'

It tastes like shit.
إنه فظيع
innahu fazii'

The spoken Arabic term for "shit" (kharaa) is not used frequently as it has strong negative (even impolite) connotations.

Water, water! maa', maa'!
ماء، ماء

My mouth's on fire. famii yahtariq
فمي يحترق

How do you eat this? kayfa ta'kul haadha?
كيف تأكل هذا ؟

Please bring me a fork. arjuuk ahdir lii shawka
أرجوك احضر لي شوكة

Do you want a knife? hal turiid sikkiin?
هل تريد سكينا ؟

I Like It!

I like this. yu'jibunii haadha
يعجبني هذا

Arab people tend to always indicate that they like things (gifts) even if they don't really think so. This is a face-saving strategy aimed at making the other person feel good about their choice of things / gifts etc.

I like it a lot. yu'jibunii kathiiran
يعجبني كثيرا

I don't like it very much. laa yu'jibunii kathiiran
لا يعجبني كثيرا

I don't like it. haadha laa yu'jibunii
هذا لا يعجبني

I hate it. akrahuh
أكرهه

I really hate it. haqiiqatan akrahuh
حقيقة أكرهه

No, thank you. laa, shukran
لا ، شكرا

I want...(noun). uriidu...
أريد...

I don't want... laa uriidu...
لا أريد...

I want to...(verb). uriidu an...
أريد أن...

I don't want to... laa uriidu an...
لا أريد أن...

I really don't want it. haqiiqatan, laa uriiduhu
حقيقة لا أريدة

I don't need this. laa ahtaaj ila haadha
لا أحتاج إلى هذا

I'm busy. anaa mashghuul
أنا مشغول

I'm happy. anaa sa'iid
أنا سعيد

I'm pleased to hear that. anaa sa'iid lisamaa' dhaalik
أنا سعيد لسماع ذلك

I'm glad to know that. anaa sa'iid lima'rifati dhaalik
أنا سعيد لمعرفة ذلك

I'm sad. anaa haziin
أنا حزين

I'm fine. anaa bikhayr
أنا بخير

I'm afraid.
أنا خائف
anaa khaa'if

I'm getting sick of it.
بدأت أمل من ذلك
bada'tu amull min dhaalik

I'm irritated.
أنا متضايق
anaa mutadaayiq

I'm mad at you.
أنا منزعج منك
anaa munza'ij minka

I'm pissed off.
أنا منزعج
anaa munza'ij

There is no equivalence in Arabic to the English "pissed off". Therefore, an alternative expression such as "munza'ij" should be used.

I'm confused.
أنا مرتبك
anaa murtabik

I'm going crazy.
سأجن
sa'ujann

I freaked.
أنا خائف
anaa khaa'if

I'm ready.
أنا مستعد
anaa musta'idd

I'm tired.
أنا تعبان
anaa ta'baan

I'm sleepy.
أنا نعسان
anaa na'saan

I'm hung over. — anaa thamil
أنا ثمل

It's not typical of people in the Arab world to indicate that they are "drunk" or "stoned". This is because drinking is not socially accepted.

I'm stoned. — anaa sakraan
أنا سكران

I'm surprised. — laqad fuuji'tu bi-haadha
لقد فوجئت بهذا

I'm bored. — ash'uru bil-malal
أشعر بالملل

I'm tired of it. — anaa mut'ab min dhaalik
أنا متعب من ذلك

What a drag! — taala haadha al-'amr 'akthar mina al-laazim
طال هذا الأمر أكثر من اللازم

How awful! — yaa lal-fazaa'a (lil-shanaa'a)
يا للفظاعة (للشناعة)

What a pity! — yaa lal-khasaara
يا للخسارة

What a relief! — lihusn il-hazz
لحسن الحظ

I'm relieved to hear that. — irtahtu lisamaa'i dhaalik
ارتحت لسماع ذلك

I feel sick. — ash'uru bit-taqayyu'
أشعر بالتقيؤ

That's sickening. هذا فظيع	haa<u>dh</u>aa fa<u>z</u>ii'
I'm disappointed. خاب أملي	<u>kh</u>aaba 'amalii
I'm disappointed in you. خاب أملي بك	<u>kh</u>aaba 'amalii bik
I was worried. كنت قلقا	kuntu qaliqan
Can you do it? أستطيع أن تفعله؟	atasta<u>t</u>ii' an taf'aluh?
I can do it. أستطيع أن أفعله	asta<u>t</u>ii' an 'af'aluh
I can't do it. لا أستطيع أن أفعله	laa asta<u>t</u>ii' an 'af'aluh
I'll do it. سأفعله	sa-'af'aluh

In Arabic such utterances are always followed with the "in<u>sh</u>a'a Allah" expression. This means "God willing".

I've got to do it. علي أن أفعله	'alayya an 'af'aluh
Sorry. آسف	aasif
I can't help it. لا أستطيع تجنب ذلك	laa astatii' tajannub <u>dh</u>aalik
That can't be helped. لا يمكن مساعدة ذلك	laa yumkin musaa'adat <u>dh</u>aalik
I understand. أنا أفهم	anaa 'afham
I know. أنا أعرف/أعلم	anaa 'a'rif / 'a'lam
I know that person. أعرف ذلك الشخص	a'rif <u>dh</u>aalika a<u>sh</u>-<u>sh</u>a<u>khs</u>

Do you know that?
أتعلم ذلك؟
ata'lam dhaalik?

Ah, you know that.
حسنا ، أنت تعلم ذلك
hasanan, anta ta'lam dhaalik

Give me time to think it over.
أعطني وقتا للتفكير بذلك
a'tinii waqtan lit-tafkiir bidhaalik

I'll think about it.
سأفكر بذلك
sa'ufakkir bidhaalik

I made a mistake.
أخطأت
akhta'tu

I blew it.
لقد أسأت التصرف
laqad asa'tu at-tasarruf

Am I right?
هل أنا على حق؟
hal anaa 'ala haqq?

Am I wrong?
هل أنا على خطأ؟
hal anaa 'ala khata'?

Curses and Insults 9

What do you want?
ماذا تريد؟
maadha turiid?

Do you want to say something?
أتريد أن تقول شيئا؟
aturiid an taquula shay-an?

Don't look at me.
لا تنظر إلي
laa tanzur ilayya

What are you staring at?
بماذا تحدق؟
bi-maadha tuhaddiq?

What did you say?
ماذا قلت؟
maadha qult?

Who do you think you're talking to?
من تعتقد أنك تخاطب؟
man ta'taqid annaka tukhaatib?

Do you know who I am?
أتعرف من أنا؟
ata'rif man anaa?

Why do you talk like that?
لماذا تتكلم هكذا؟
limaadha tatakallam haakadha?

Come here, I'll teach you some manners.
تعال إلى هنا، سأعلمك بعض الآداب
ta'aal ila huna, sa'u'allimuka ba'da al-aadab

Don't mess round with me.
لا تتلاعب معي
laa tatalaa'ab ma'ii

Stop it!
توقف
tawaqqaf!

Shut up!
أسكت
uskut!

What are you doing?
ماذا تفعل؟
maadha taf'al?

What did you hit me for?
لماذا تضربني؟
limaadha tadribunii?

Why did you push me?
لماذا دفعتني؟
limaadha dafa'tanii?

Do you want to fight?
أتريد أن تتشاجر؟
aturiid an tatashaajar?

I'm going to kill you.
سأقتلك
sa'aqtuluk

Are we going to fight or not?
هل سنتشاجر أم لا؟
hal sa-natashaajar am laa?

Let's fight and see.
هيا نتشاجر وسنرى
hayya natashaajar wa sa-naraa.

Ouch!
آه!
aah!

That hurts.
هذا يؤلم
haadha yu'lim

Don’t! — laa taf’al
لا تفعل

Don’t hit me. — laa tadribnii
لا تدربني

Don’t do it again. — laa taf’aal dhaalik marra ukhra
لا تفعل ذلك مرة أخرى

Help! — an-najda!
النجدة

You’re making me laugh. — innaka tudhikunii
إنك تضحكني

You deserve it. — tastahiq dhaalik
تستحق ذلك

You win. — anta l-faa'iz
أنت الفائز

You’re right. — anta ’ala haqq
أنت على حق

I was wrong. — kuntu mukhti'
كنت مخطيء

It was my fault. — kaanaat ghaltatii
كانت غلطتي

Forgive me. — saamihnii
سامحني

Say you’re sorry. — qul innaka muta'assif
قل إنك متأسف

I’m sorry. — anaa aasif
أنا آسف

I forgive you. — saamahtuka
سامحتك

You’re stupid. — anta ahmaq
أنت أحمق

That’s stupid. — haadhihi hamaaqa
هذه حماقة

What you did was stupid. — maa fa'altahu kaana humqan
ما فعلته كان حمقا

You're crazy. — anta majnuun
أنت مجنون

Liar! — kadhdhaab!
كذاب

You've got a big mouth! — anta tatakallam kathiiran (mishkaljii)!
أنت تتكلم كثيرا

Get your head out of your ass! — kun fii l-mustawa!
كن في المستوى

This is not a literal translation of the English sentence, which does not have an exact equivalent in Arabic. However, it conveys a similar meaning.

You bitch! — yaa 'aahira!
يا ابن العاهرة!

This term is not used as easily as it is in English and other European languages. It reflects poorly on the speaker as much as on the person in question.

You bastard! — yaa l-'aahira!
يا ابن العاهرة!

The note above also applies with this expression.

Shorty! — yaa qasiir!
يا قصير

Fatty! — yaa samiin!
يا سمين

Being moderately "fat" is not viewed negatively in the Arab world. On the contrary, it is a sign that one is happy, well off, and well-looked after (well fed).

Four-eyes! — yaa abuu n-nazzaraat!
يا ابو النظارات

Weakling! — yaa lad-du'f!
يا للضعف

You ain't got balls!
ليس لديك الشجاعة الكافية
laysa ladayka ash-shajaa'a al-kaafiya!

Your tool is small!
يا صغير القضيب!
yaa saghiir l-qadiib!

Such explicit reference to someone's "tool" is not a common thing in Arabic, and should be avoided...

You're ugly!
أنت قبيح!
anta qabiih!

You're the lowest!
أنت عديم الأصل
anta 'adiim t-asil!

Don't be so cocky!
لا تكن مغرورا!
laa takun maghruuran!

You're a tightwad!
يا بخيل!
yaa bakhiil!

Arabs value generosity, and to label someone a "tightwad" is extremely offensive.

Go to hell!
أغرب عني!
ughrub 'annii!

Fuck you!!
أغرب عني!
ughrub 'annii!

The f-word is not used in Arabic in the same way it is in English. The alternative listed here coveys a similarly strong message without the inherently offensive nature of the f-word.

Take your hands off!
إرفع يديك عني!
irfa' yadayka 'annii!

Don't touch me!
لا تلمسني!
laa talmusnii!

I think you're trying to trick me.
أظن انك تحاول أن تخدعني
azunnu annaka tuhaawil an takhda'nii

This can't be so expensive.
لا يمكن أن يكون هذا غاليا بهذا الشكل
laa yumkin an yakuun haadha ghaaliyan bihaadhaa ash-shakl

This is different from what I've heard.
هذا يختلف عما سمعت
haadha yakhtalif 'ammaa sami't!

If you think I don't know anything, you're wrong.
إذا ظننت أنني لا أعلم شيئا فأنت مخطيء
idhaa zanaanta annii laa a'lam shay-an fa-anta mukhti'

Don't think I'm stupid.
لا تظن أني أحمق
laa tazunn annii 'ahmaq

Explain to me why.
إشرح لي لماذا
ishrah lii limaadhaa

Think about it.
فكر بهذا الأمر
fakkir bihaadha l-'amr

Don't you think you're wrong?
ألا تظن أنك مخطيء؟
alaa tazunn annaka mukhti'?

I want to talk to the manager.
أريد أن أتكلم مع المدير
uriidu an atakallama ma'a l-mudiir

I'll never come here again.
لن آتي إلى هنا مرة أخرى
lan aatii ila hunaa marra ukhraa

I'll tell all my friends.
سأخبر جميع أصدقائي
sa-'ukhbir jamii' asdiqaa'ii

Tell me your name!
قلي ما إسمك
qullii maa ismuk!

You'd better remember what you tried to do.
الأفضل أن تتذكر ما حاولت أن تفعل
al'afdal an tatadhakkar maa haawalta an taf'al

Party Talk 10

Do you come here often?
هل تأتي إلى هنا عادة؟
hal ta'tii ila huna 'aadatan?

To start a conversation with people you don't know, it is normal for people in the Arab countries to ask about your native country occupation, hobbies etc...

Have I seen you before?
هل تقابلنا من قبل؟
hal taqaabalna min qabl?

Are you having a good time?
هل تتسلى جيدا ؟
hal tatasallaa jayyidan?

You look like you're having a good time.
يبدو أنك تقضي وقتا جيدا
yabduu annaka taqdii waqtan jayyidan

Yes, I'm having fun.
نعم، أنا أتسلى
na'am, anaa atasallaa

We're having a good time, aren't we?
نحن نقضي وقتا ممتعا ، أليس كذلك؟
nahnu naqdii waqtan mumti'an, alaysa kadhaalik?

This place is fun.
هذا المكان جيد للتسلية
haadha l-makaan jayyid lit-tasliya

Can I join you?
هل أستطيع أن أشاركك؟
hal astatii' an ushaarikak?

Although socializing and entertaining guests is a high priority in most Arab countries, it is still essential to check that you are indeed welcome to join in.

Shall we drink together?

ما رأيك في أن نتناول مشروبا ؟
maa ra'yuka fii an natanaawala mashruuban?

Sometimes it is normal for someone to buy a drink (tea / coffee, soft drink, etc.) before checking whether you actually want it or not.

Can I buy you a drink?
هل أستطيع أن أشتري لك مشروبا ؟
astatii' an ashtarii laka mashruuban?

Can I sit here?
هل أستطيع أن أجلس هنا ؟
hal astatii' an ajlisa huna?

Has someone reserved this seat?
هل هذا المقعد محجوز؟
hal haadha l-maq'ad mahjuuz?

Is someone sitting here?
هل من شخص يجلس هنا ؟
hal min shakhs yajlis huna?

Someone's sitting here.
نعم شخص يجلس هنا
na'am shakhsun yajlis huna

Do you want to sit down?
هل تريد أن تجلس؟
hal turiid an tajlis?

May I sit down?
هل أستطيع أن أجلس؟
hal astatii' an ajlis?

Please sit down. — ijlis min fadlik
أجلس من فضلك

Scoot over. — iqtarib qaliilan
إقترب قليلا

What did you say? — maadha qult?
ماذا قلت؟

What's your name? — maa asmuk?
ما أسمك؟

My name's... — ismii...
اسمي...

When someone introduces himself, it is customary to reply with the expression "tacharrafna", meaning "honored to meet you". This is so even in the most informal gatherings.

Guess what it is! — ahzir maa haadhaa!
أحزر ما هذا

Are you here alone? — hal anta wahdaka huna?
هل أنت وحدك هنا؟

Yes, I'm here alone. — na'am, anaa huna wahdii
نعم، أنا هنا وحدي

No, I'm here with my friends. — laa, anaa huna ma' asdiqaa'ii
لا، أنا هنا مع أصدقائي

Did you two come here together? — hal ji'tumaa ma'an?
هل جئتما معا؟

Where do you live? — ayna taskun?
أين تسكن؟

Where do you come from? min ayna ant?
من أين أنت؟

How long have you been in this country? mundhu mata hadrat ila haadhihi l-bilaad?
منذ متى حضرت إلى هذه البلاد ؟

Do you like Arab guys / girls? hal yu'jibuka sh-shabaab / l-banaaat al-'arab?
هل يعجبك الشباب/البنات العرب؟

This is a common question that should be answered diplomatically with the word "na'am" word meaning "yes".

How old are you? kam 'umruk?
كم عمرك؟

Unlike in Western cultures, it is not offensive in Arabic culture to ask both men and women about their ages.

Are you a student? hal anta taalib?
هل أنت طالب؟

Your English is good. lughatuka l-inkliiziyya jayyida
لغتك الإنكليزية جيدة

What's your job? maa hiya waziifatuka ('amaluk)?
ما هي وظيفتك (عملك) ؟

That's an interesting job. innaha waziifa muthiira lil-ihtimaam
إنها وظيفة مثيرة للإهتمام

Where do you work? ayna ta'mal?
أين تعمل؟

How do you spend your time? kayfa taqdii waqtak?
كيف تقضي وقتك؟

What kinds of hobbies do you have? maa hiya hiwaayaatuk?
ما هي هوأياتك؟

What music do you like? maa hiya l-muusiiqaa l-latii tu'jibuk?
ما هي الموسيقى التي تعجبك؟

Do you know this song? ata'rif haa<u>dh</u>ihi l-'u<u>gh</u>niya?
أتعرف هذه الأغنية؟

I know it. a'rifuhaa
أعرفها

I don't know it. laa a'rifuhaa
لا أعرفها

This is the first time I'm hearing it. haa<u>dh</u>ihi awwalu marra asma'u <u>dh</u>aalik
هذه أول مرة أسمع ذلك

Shall we dance? mumkin an narqu<u>s</u>?
ممكن أن نرقص؟

I can't dance.
لا أجيد الرقص
laa ujiidu r-raqsa

Are you in the mood?
هل لديك الرغبة؟
hal ladayka r-raghba?

Not really.
الحقيقة لا
al-haqiiqa laa

I don't feel like dancing yet.
لست راغبا في الرقص بعد
lastu raaghiban fil-raqs ba'd

You're a good dancer.
أنت تجيد الرقص
anta tujiid r-raqsa

Complimenting others, even when the compliment is a little too generous, is important in Arabic culture.

How do you know of this place?
كيف عرفت هذا المكان؟
kayfa 'arifta haadha l-makaan?

I heard from my friends.
سمعت من أصدقائي
sami'tu min asdiqaa'ii

Where else do you go to dance?
إلى أي أماكن أخرى تذهب للرقص؟
ila 'ayyi amaakinin 'ukhra tadhhab lir-raqs?

Let's party!
هيا نحتفل
hayya nahtafil!

Let's get drunk!
هيا نسكر
hayya naskar!

What are you drinking?
ماذا تشرب؟
maadhaa tashrab?

Have you been drinking a lot?
هل شربت كثيرا ؟
hal sharibta kathiiran?

Well, drink some more!
حسنا ، أشرب المزيد
hasanaan, ishrab l-maziid!

You need to drink more.
أنت تحتاج أن تشرب المزيد
anta tahtaaj an tashrab l-maziid

You're a strong drinker.
أنت شريب
anta shirriib

Are you drunk?
هل أنت سكران؟
hal anta sakraan?

Haven't you drunk too much?
ألا تعتقد أنك شربت كثيرا ؟
alaa ta'taqid annaka sharibta kathiiran?

Maybe you should stop drinking.
من الأفضل أن تتوقف عن الشرب
mina l-afdal an tatawaqqafa 'an sh-shurb

Are you OK?
هل أنت على مايرام؟
hal anta 'ala maa yuraam?

What time did you come here?
متى جئت إلى هنا ؟
mata ji'ta ila huna?

What time do you have to be home?
متى تعود إلى البيت؟
mata ta'uud ila l-bayt?

What time are you leaving?
متى ستغادر ؟
mata sa-tughaadir?

It depends.
يتوقف على
yatawaqqaf 'ala

If I have a good time, I'll stay.
إذا كنت أتسلى جيدا ، سأبقى
idhaa kuntu atasalla jayyidan, sa'abqaa

If this gets boring, I'll go home.
إذا ضجرت، سأغادر
idhaa dajirt, sa-ughaadir

I'll help you to have a good time.
سأساعدك لتقضي وقتا جميلا
sa'usaa'iduka litaqdii waqtan jamiilan

What's next?
ماذا بعد ذلك؟
maadha ba'da dhaalik?

Shall we leave?
هل نغادر؟
hal nughaadir?

Shall we go somewhere else?
هل نذهب إلى مكان آخر؟
hal nadhhab ila makaanin aakhar?

Can my friends come?
هل يستطيع أصدقائي أن يأتوا؟
hal yastatii' asdiqaa'ii an ya'tuu?

Where shall we go?
إلى أين نذهب؟
ila ayna nadhhab?

What shall we do?
ماذا نفعل؟
maadhaa naf'al?

It's up to you.
حسب رغبتك
hasaba raghbatik

Anywhere's OK.
أي مكان جيد
ayya makaanin jayyid

I'd like to stay here longer.
أرغب في أن أبقى هنا لفترة أطول
arghabu fii an abqaa huna lifatra atwal

Don't go yet.
لا تذهب بعد
laa tadhhab ba'd

Go later.
أذهب فيما بعد
idhhab fiimaa ba'd

I'll take you home.
سآخذك إلى البيت
sa-aakhudhuka ila l-bayt

Do you want to come to my place?
أتريد أن تأتي إلى بيتي؟
aturiidu an ta'ti ila baytii?

I'm not sure.
لست متأكدة
lastu muta'akkida

Just for coffee.
فقط لشرب القهوة
faqat lishurb l-qahwa

Yes, let's go.
نعم، هيابنا
na'am, hayyaa binaa

Getting Serious 11

I want to know more about you.
أريد أن أعرفك أكثر
uriidu an a'rifaka akthar

Getting to know a potential partner (girlfriend / boyfriend) in terms of their background, family, work, etc. is essential before the relationship can become closer.

I want to know all about you.
أريد أن أعرف كل شيء عنك
uriidu an a'rifa kul shay' 'ank

I'll tell you.
سأقول لك
sa-aquulu laka

Shall we meet again?
هل ممكن أن نلتقي مرة أخرى؟
hal mumkin an naltaqya marra ukhraa?

When can I see you next time?
متى أستطيع أن أراك مرة أخرى؟
mata astatii' an araaka marra ukhraa?

May I call you?
هل ممكن أن أتصل بك؟
hal mumkin an attasila bik?

Calling someone at home is not always a straightforward issue if you have not been introduced to the family. This is especially true for calling girls at their home numbers.

May I have your phone number?
هل ممكن أن أحصل على رقم هاتفك؟
hal mumkin an ahsula 'ala raqim haatifik?

Here's my phone number.
هذا هو رقم هاتفي
haadha huwa raqim haatifii

Do you have something to write with?
هل لديك قلما ؟
hal ladayka qalaman?

Will you call me?
هل ستتصل بي؟
hal sa-tattasil bii?

I enjoyed myself.
لقد أستمتعت كثيرا
laqad istamta'tu kathiiran

It was fun.
كان مسليا
kaana musalliyan

Take care.
كن حذرا
kun hadhiran

See you later.
إلى اللقاء
ila al-liqaa'

See you tomorrow.
أراك غدا
araaka ghadan

Hello.
مرحبا
marhaban

Is Mary at home?
هل ماري في البيت؟
hal Mary fil-bayt?

Hold on please.
إنتظر أرجوك
intazir arjuuk

Mary, telephone!
ماري تليفون!
Mary, tilifuun!

Mary is out.
ماري ليست هنا
Mary laysat hunaa

Please tell her I called.
أرجو أن تخبرها أنني إتصلت
arjuu an tukhbirhaa annanii ittasalt.

This is Robert.
هذا روبرت
haadha Robert

Are you doing OK?
هل أنت على ما يرام؟
hal anta 'ala maa yuraam?

What have you been doing?
ماذا كنت تفعل؟
maadha kunta taf'al?

I've missed you.
إشتقت إليك
ishtaqtu ilayk

I've been thinking of you.
كنت أفكر بك
kuntu ufakkiru bika

I want to see you.
أريد أن أراك
uriidu an araaka

Shall we meet now?
ممكن أن نلتقي الآن؟
mumkin an naltaqii al-aan?

I can't go out now.
لا استطيع أن أخرج الآن
laa astatii' an akhruja ala'an

Going out (for girls) can be a tricky affair as it has to be authorized by parents and / or other family members. However, if a group of friends are to go out together during reasonable hours, then it should not be a difficult occasion to organise.

I'll call you again.
سأتصل بك مرة أخرى
sa-attasil bika marra ukhra

I'll call you tomorrow at six o'clock.
سأتصل بك غدا الساعة السادسة
sa-attasil bika ghadan as-saa'a as-saadisa

Please be in.
أرجوك كن في البيت
arjuuk kun fil-bayt

I'll write you a letter.
سأكتب لك رسالة
sa-aktub laka risaala

Will you write me a letter?
هل ستكتب لي رسالة؟
hal sataktub lii risaala?

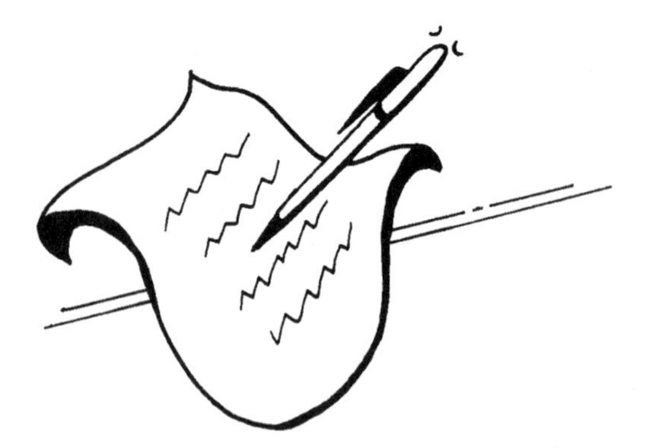

I'll call you from America.
سأتصل بك من أمريكا
sa-attasil bika min amriikaa

I'll call you when I return.
سأتصل بك عندما أعود ؟
sa-attasil bika 'indamaa a'uud

I'll be back soon.
سأعود قريبا
sa-a'uud qariiban

Do you have to go?
هل يجب أن تذهب الأن؟
hal yajib an tadhhab al-aan?

Please don't go.
أرجوك لا تذهب
arjuuk laa tadhhab

Stay here with me.
إبق هنا معي
ibqa huna ma'ii

Please understand.
أرجوك كن متفهما
arjuuk kun mutafahim

I have to go because it's my job.
يجب أن أذهب بسبب وظيفتي (عملي)
yajib an adhhaba bisabab waziifatii ('amalii)

Take care of your health.
انتبه إلى صحتك
intabih ila sihhatik

Please wait for my return.
أرجوك أنتظرني حتى أعود
arjuuk intazirnii hatta a'uud

Don't cry.
لاتبك
laa tabki

Wipe your tears.
إمسح دموعك/إمسحي دموعك
imsah dumuu'ak / imsahii dumuu'aki

I can't stand it! laa astatii' an ahtamil dhaalik!
لا أستطيع أن أحتمل ذلك

It's difficult for me too. innahu sa'bun 'alayya aydan
إنه صعب علي أيضا

Lovers' Language 12

I love you. uhibbuk
أحبك

Declaring one's love does not happen rapidly. It takes a rather long time before one is able to utter such statements as they indicate a long-term commitment beyond the immediate future.

I'm crazy about you. anaa majnuun bihubbik
أنا مجنون بحبك

I'm yours. anaa kullii lak
أنا كلي لك

You're mine. anti mulkii
أنت ملكي

You look beautiful. anti jamiila
أنت جميلة

You look handsome. anta wasiim
أنت وسيم

It is common for women to compliment men, but not too excessively.

You're attractive.
أنت جذابة
anti jadhaaba

You're sexy.
جمالك مثير جدا
jamaaluki muthiir jiddan

You have beautiful eyes / lips/ hands / teeth / legs / breasts.
عيناك / شفتاك / يداك / أسنانك / ساقاك / ثديك جميلة
'aynaaki / shafataaki / yadaaki / asnaanik / saaqaaki / thadyaki jamiil(a)

Your face / nose / neck is lovely.
وجهك / أنفك / رقبتك جميل
wajhuk / anfuk / raqbatuk jamiil

You have a beautiful body.
أنت رشيقة القوام
anti rashiiqata l-qawaam

You smell sweet.
رائحتك طيبة
ra'ihatuki tayyiba

May I kiss you?
هل لي أن أقبلك؟
hal lii an uqabbiluk?

Kiss me.
قبلني
qabbilnii

Girls in most Arab countries show a lot of modesty when it comes to dis-playing physical affection. It is rare for them to ask explicitly for "kisses".

Where?
أين؟
ayna?

I want to hold your hand.
أريد أن أمسك يدك
uriidu an umsika yadik

Look into my eyes.
أنظري في عيني
unzurii fii 'aynay

Come closer to me.
إقتربي مني
iqtaribii minnii

Hug me.
أحضني
uhdunnii

Take your clothes off.
إخلعي ملابسك الداخلية
ikhla'ii malaabisik ad-daakhiliyya

Take your shoes / socks / shirt / jeans off.
إخلع حذائك/جواربك/قميصك/سروالك
ikhla' hidha'auk / jawaaribik / qamiisik / sirwaalik

Take your dress / bra / panties off.
إخلعي فستانك/صدريتك/ملابسك الداخلية
ikhla'ii fustaanik / sidriyyatik / malaabisik ad-daakhiliyya

I'm cold.
أنا بردان
anaa bardaan

Make me warm.
دفئني
daffi'nii

That tickles.
هذا يدغدغ
hadhaa yudaghdigh

I want to see your...
أريد أن أرى...
uriidu an araa...

I want to kiss your...
أريد أن أقبل...
uriidu an uqabbil...

I want to suck your...
أريد أن أمص...
uriidu an amuss...

Such explicit language is not common among Arabic lovers.

knees
الركبة
ar-rukba

toes
أصابع القدم
asaabi' l-qadam

thing
شيء
shay'

breasts
ثدي
thadii

nipples
الحلمات
al-halmaat

pussy
المهبل
al-mahbal

butt
المؤخرة
al-mu'akhira

dick
قضيب
qadiib

balls
خشيتان
khisyataan

Do you want to have sex?
هل تريد أن تمارس الجنس معي؟
hal turiid an tumaarisa l-jins ma'ii?

I'm embarrassed.
أنا خجلانة
anaa khajlaana

Don't be shy.
لا تخجل
laa takhjal

Close your eyes.
أغلق عينيك
aghliq 'aynayk

Turn off the light.
أطفئ النور
atfi' an-nuur

Look the other way for a second.
أنظر إلى الجانب الآخر للحظة
unzur ila l-jaanib l-aakhar lilahza

Is this your first time?
هل هذه أول مرة لك؟
hal haadhihi awwal marra lak?

Tell me the truth.
قل الحقيقة
qul l-haqiiqa

I'm still a virgin.
ما زلت عذراء
maa ziltu 'adhraa'

Virginity is very important for girls in the Arab / Muslim world. A girl is not meant to lose her virginity before marriage.

I'm frightened.
أنا خائفة
anaa khaa'ifa

Don't worry.
لا تقلقي
laa taqlaqii

It's going to be OK.
كل شيء سيكون على ما يرام
kul shay' sayakuun 'ala maa yuraam

I'll be careful.
سأكون حذرا
saakuun hadhiran

Treat me gently.
عاملني بلطف
'aamilnii bilutf

I'm afraid I'll get pregnant.
أخشى أن أحمل
akhsha an ahmil

I don't want to have a baby.
لا أريد أطفالا الآن
laa uriidu atfaalan al-aan

Will you use protection?
هل ستستعمل الواقي؟
hal satasta'mil l-waaqii?

Another word for "condom" is "al-kabuut".

I don't like to wear a condom.
لا أحب استعمال الواقي
laa uhibb isti'maal l-waaqii

If you don't wear a condom, I won't do it.
إذا لم تستعمل الواقي، فلن أمارس الجنس معك
idhaa lam tasta'mil l-waaqii, falan umaaris l-jins ma'ak

Are you on the pill?
هل تتناولي حبوب منع الحمل؟
hal tatanaawalii hubuub man' l-hamal

Is today safe for you?
هل اليوم مناسب لك؟
hal l-yawm munaasib lak?

I want you.
أريدك
uriiduk

It's been a long time.
لم أمارس الجنس منذ مدة
lam umaaris l-jins mundhu mudda

How do you want me to do it?
كيف تفضلين ممارست الجنس؟
kayfa tufaddiliin mumarasat l-jins?

I feel so good.
أشعر بالسعادة
ash'ur bis-sa'aada

Touch me.
المسني
ilmisnii

Bite me.
عضني
'uddanii

Love me more.
أحبني أكثر
ahibbanii akthir

More and more.
أكثر فأكثر
akthar fa-akthar

Do the same thing again.
كرر نفس الشيء
karrir nafsa sh-shay'

Stronger. بشكل أقوى	bi-shakl aqwaa
Softer. بلطف	bi-lutf
Faster. أسرع	asra'
Slower. ببطء	bi-but'
Deeper. أعمق	a'maq
I'm coming. لقد وصلت الذروة	laqad wasaltu adh-dharwa
Wait, wait! إنتظر، إنتظر	intazir, intazir!
Did you like that? هل أعجبك ذلك؟	hal a'jabaki dhaalik?
Did you come? هل وصلت الذروة؟	hal wasalta dh-dharwa?
I came. نعم، وصلت الذروة	na'am, wasaltu dh-dharwa
That was good. كان ذلك جيدا	kaana dhaalika jayyidan
That was wonderful. كان ذلك رائعا	kaana dhaalika raa'i'an
I don't want to leave you. لا أريد أن أتركك	laa uriidu an atrukak

This is an indication of strong attachment and serious intentions. It should be taken very seriously.

I want to stay with you forever. uriidu an abqaa ma'ak lil'abad
أريد أن أبقى معك للأبد

One more time? marra ukhra?
مرة أخرى؟

The Other Side 13

Will you marry me?
هل تتزوجني/هل تتزوجيني؟
hal tatazawwajanii / hal atatazawwajiinii?

Popping the question in the Arab world takes place formally at the family level. Nowadays, this follows a period of semi-formal dating / engagement which normally leads to marriage.

Let's get married.
هيا فلنتزوج
hayya fa-li-natazawwaj

I want to be your wife / husband.
أريد أن أكون زوجتك/زوجك
uriidu an akuuna zawjataka / zawjaki

Will you come to America / Australia / Europe with me?
هل تأتين معي إلى أمريكا/أستراليا/أوروبا؟
hal ta'tiina ma'ii ila amriikaa / ustraaliya / urubaa?

Young people in the Arab world are not free to travel overseas unless this is sanctioned by their families and is specifically related to work, study or other family business.

I want to stay in this country.
أريد أن أبقى في هذا البلد
uriidu an abqaa fii haadha al-balad

I don't want to leave my family.
لا أريد أن أترك عائلتي
laa uriidu an atruka 'aa'ilatii

I don't want to get married yet.
لا أريد أن أتزوج بعد
laa uriidu an atazawwaja ba'du

I don't want to get engaged yet.
لا أريد أن أخطب بعد
laa uriidu an akhtuba ba'du

I don't want to think about marriage yet.
لا أريد أن أفكر في الزواج بعد
laa uriidu an ufakkira fiz-zawaaj ba'du

I'm too young.
أنا صغير جدا في السن
anaa saghiir jiddan fi s-sinn

It's not time for me to get serious.
هذا ليس وقت الأمور الجدية
haadha laysa waqt al-umuur al-jiddiyya

I love you but I can't marry you.
أحبك لكن لا أستطيع أن أتزوجك
uhibbuka laakin laa astatii' an atazawwajak

I'm already married.
أنا متزوج
anaa mutazawwij

Married people (in particular women) do not enter in extra-marital affairs as this brings shame onto them and their families.

I need time to myself.
أحتاج وقتا لنفسي
ahtaaju waqtan linafsii

I need time to think.
أحتاج وقتا لأفكر
ahtaaju waqtan li'ufakkir

This is so sudden.
هذا مفاجئ
haadha mufaaji'

We must think about this.
يجب أن نفكر بذلك
yajib an nufakkira bi-dhaalik

You don't love me any more, do you?
لم تعد تحبني أبدا ، أليس هذا صحيحا ؟
lam ta'ud tuhibbunii abadan, alaysa haadha sahiihan?

Do you have another girlfriend / boyfriend?
هل لديك صديق أخر / صديقة أخرى ؟
hal ladayka sadiiq aakhar / sadiiqa ukhraa?

Please tell me, I want to know.
أرجوك أخبرني، أريد أن أعرف
arjuuka akhbirnii, uriidu an a'rifa

Let's not see each other again.
لنتوقف عن رؤية بعضنا
li-natawaqqaf 'an ru'yat ba'dina

I can't see you anymore.
لا أستطيع أن أراك في المستقبل
laa astatii' an araak fii l-mustaqbal

I have another girlfriend / boyfriend.
عندي صديق آخر/صديقة أخرى
'indii sadiiq aakhar / sadiiqa ukhraa

I like you, but I don't love you anymore.
أنت تعجبني ولكنني لم أعد أحبك
anta tu'jibnii wa laakinnii lam a'ud uhibbuk

I'm not interested in you anymore.
لم يعد لدي أي إهتمام بك
lam ya'ud ladayya ayy ihtimaam bik.

Being with you is no fun. wujuudii ma'ak lam ya'ud musalliyan.
وجودي معك لم يعد مسليا

You're boring! anta mumill!
أنت ممل

This is strong statement that indicates genuine dislike.

I hate you! akrahuka!
أكرهك

Same as above.

I'm not good for you. anaa ghayru munaasib lak.
أنا غير مناسب لك

This is a more acceptable way of indicating a break-up.

Forget about me. insaanii
انساني

I'm sorry it didn't work out. aasif li-ann al-mawduu' lam yatimm
أسف لأن الموضوع لم يتم

It's over. intahaa al-mawduu'
إنتهى الموضوع

I won't call you any more. lan attasila bika ba'da al-aan
لن أتصل بك بعد الآن

Don't call me again. laa tatasil bii ba'da al-aan
لا تتصل بي بعد الآن

I'm going to change my phone number. sawfa ughayyir raqma haatifii
سوف أغير رقم هاتفي

Don't be persistent. laa takun musirran
لا تكن مصرا

Stop bothering me. tawaqqaf 'an iza'aajii
توقف عن ازعاجي

It is an unacceptable offence to persist in calling a girl if she indicates that she does not want to continue the relationship. If the family becomes aware of such harassment then the consequences could be serious.

Get lost! insarif min hunaa!
انصرف من هنا

I'm sorry I haven't been a good girlfriend / boyfriend. aasif li'anii lam akun sadiiqan jayyidan
آسف لأني لم أكن صديق جيد

It's my fault. haadha khata'ii
هذا خطئي

Can't we start again? alaa nastatii' an nabda'a min jadiid?
ألا نستطيع أن نبدأ من جديد؟

Forget it! insaa dhaalika!
إنسى ذلك

I'm serious about you. anaa atakallam bijiddiya.
أنا أتكلم بجدية

I can't live without you. laa astatii'u an a'iisha biduunik
لا أستطيع أن أعيش بدونك

Please understand my feelings. arjuuka tafahham mashaa'irii
أرجوك تفهم مشاعري

I'll miss you.
سأشتاق إليك
sa-ashtaaqu ilayk

I'll never forget you.
لن أنساك أبدا
lan ansaak abadan.

Thanks for the beautiful memories.
أشكرك على الذكريات الجميلة
ashkuruk 'alaa adh-dhikrayaat al-jamiila.

I'm so happy to have known you.
أنا سعيد جدا لأني عرفتك
anaa sa'iidun jiddan li'annii 'araftuk

Remember me sometimes.
تذكرني بين الحين والآخر
tadhakkarnii bayn l-hiin wa l-aakhar.

Can we still be friends?
هل ممكن أن نبقى أصدقاء؟
hal mumkin an nabqaa asdiqaa'?

Be happy with her / him.
أتمنى لك السعادة معه/أتمنى لك السعادة معها
atamanna laka as-saa'ada ma'ahaa / atamanna laki as-saa'ada ma'ahu.

I'll always think of you.
سأتذكرك دائما
sa-atadhakaruk daa'iman

I'll always love you.
سأحبك دائما
sa-uhibbuk daa'iman